MW01153541

CHRISTIAN PULISIC

BY TODD KORTEMEIER

WORLD'S GREATEST SOCCER PLAYERS

SportsZone

An Imprint of Abdo Publishing
abdobooks.com

abdobooks.com

Published by Abdo Publishing, a division of ABDO, PO Box 398166, Minneapolis, Minnesota 55439. Copyright © 2020 by Abdo Consulting Group, Inc. International copyrights reserved in all countries. No part of this book may be reproduced in any form without written permission from the publisher. SportsZone™ is a trademark and logo of Abdo Publishing.

Printed in the United States of America, North Mankato, Minnesota
082019
012020

THIS BOOK CONTAINS
RECYCLED MATERIALS

Cover Photo: Robin Alam/Icon Sportswire/AP Images
Interior Photos: Robin Alam/Icon Sportswire/AP Images, 4, 7, 9; Mike Carlson/Getty Images Sport/Getty Images, 10, 20; Martin Rose/FIFA/Getty Images, 13; Guido Kirchner/picture-alliance/dpa/AP Images, 15; Bernd Thissen/picture-alliance/dpa/AP Images, 16; Martin Meissner/AP Images, 18; Jay LaPrete/AP Images, 23; Ina Fassbender/picture-alliance/dpa/AP Images, 24; Robin Alam/Icon Sportswire/AP Images, 27; Mo Khursheed/TFV Media/AP Images, 28

Editor: Patrick Donnelly
Series Designer: Craig Hinton

Library of Congress Control Number: 2019942091

Publisher's Cataloging-in-Publication Data

Names: Kortemeier, Todd, author.
Title: Christian Pulisic / by Todd Kortemeier
Description: Minneapolis, Minnesota : Abdo Publishing, 2020 | Series: World's greatest soccer players | Includes online resources and index.
Identifiers: ISBN 9781532190674 (lib. bdg.) | ISBN 9781644943465 (pbk.) | ISBN 9781532176524 (ebook)
Subjects: LCSH: Soccer players--Biography--Juvenile literature. | Chelsea Football Club--Juvenile literature. | European football--Biography--Juvenile literature. | Professional athletes--Biography--Juvenile literature.
Classification: DDC 796.3340922--dc23

TABLE OF CONTENTS

AMERICAN
HERO

In June 2017, the US men's national soccer team needed a hero. The team was a mess. The Americans were trying to qualify for the 2018 World Cup. However, they had started World Cup qualifying with just one win in their first four matches.

The team's coach, Jürgen Klinsmann, had been fired. Their all-time leading scorer, Landon Donovan, had recently retired. Their second leading scorer, Clint Dempsey, was on the downside of his career. Someone had to step up. It turned out to be a teenager.

Christian Pulisic was ready to step up for the US men's national team against Trinidad and Tobago.

Christian Pulisic was just 18 years old. He had made his US senior team debut barely a year earlier. But the attacking midfielder had already scored four goals in 13 international matches. And he played for a strong club team in Germany. Fans hoped he could be the player to turn around the US fortunes.

The United States hosted Trinidad and Tobago in its next match. The Americans were expected to win. However, very little had gone as expected for the Americans during World Cup qualifying. And after a scoreless first half, the US team had plenty of work to do.

Pulisic made his move in the 52nd minute. The ball bounced out to teammate Darlington Nagbe. His options appeared limited. But Pulisic spotted an opening. He streaked toward the goal. Nagbe fired the ball his way. Pulisic, in just the right spot, slid forward and kicked the ball into the net. The United States took a 1–0 lead. Pulisic stood up and sprinted toward the US fans behind the goal. He slid again in celebration in front of the frenzied fans.

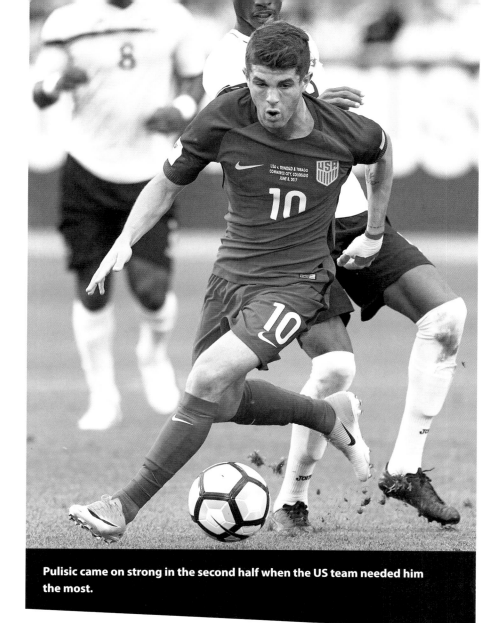

Pulisic came on strong in the second half when the US team needed him the most.

But he was not done. Ten minutes later, Pulisic passed off to a teammate and made a run toward the goal. It was the perfect move. Jozy Altidore's long pass found Pulisic open inside the box. The teenager saw a narrow opening and buried a hard shot past the goalkeeper for a 2–0 lead.

The US team held on to win by the same score. It was a massive victory. It put the United States back into position to qualify for the World Cup. There was still a long way to go. But the Americans knew they had a rising star for the future.

CROATIA OR US?

Pulisic was born in the United States. But his grandfather was born in Croatia. That meant he could play for either the US or Croatia national team. But Pulisic always dreamed of playing for his home country, so he chose the US team.

Pulisic plays to the fans after scoring against Trinidad and Tobago.

USA v. TRINIDAD & TOBAGO
COMMERCE CITY, COLORADO
JUNE 8, 2017
USA
10

PENNSYLVANIA
PRODIGY

Mark and Kelley Pulisic knew their son would be an athlete. They saw it when he was five years old. Christian was already showing signs of being a soccer star. They didn't push him to choose soccer. But given their experience with the game, it was no surprise he ended up choosing it.

Mark and Kelley both played college soccer at George Mason University in Virginia. Mark went on to a pro career playing indoor soccer. He played for a team in Harrisburg, Pennsylvania, from 1991 to 1999. Christian was born September 18, 1998, in nearby Hershey.

Christian got the chance to travel to play soccer at a young age thanks to his parents. When Christian was seven, Kelley got a teaching job in England, and the family lived near the town of Oxford for a year. Christian played soccer for a club called Brackley Town.

In 2006 the family moved to Michigan. Mark coached an indoor soccer team in Detroit called the Ignition. Christian played for the Michigan Rush, a strong youth team. By the time Christian was 10, he knew soccer was his sport.

The family soon returned to Pennsylvania, where Christian began playing for the club PA Classics. He also made his debut for the US Under-17 team when he was just 14 years old. And each summer, Christian and his dad

STRONG WILL

Christian has a cousin named Will who also plays soccer. Will Pulisic is a goalkeeper. He originally committed to play college soccer at Duke University. But in 2016, he got an offer to join his cousin at Dortmund and signed there. He played in several matches for Dortmund's youth team, then returned to the United States to play for Duke.

Christian, *left*, and his cousin Will were teammates on the US team at the U-17 World Cup in 2015.

traveled to Europe to visit some of the world's top clubs and watch them train.

Growing up, Christian was often one of the smaller players on the field. He knew he couldn't rely on size and strength as an advantage. Instead, he focused on understanding the game. He also practiced dribbling a lot, especially working on his first touch.

This hard work paid off. Christian was becoming a great player. But to get even better, he knew he had to challenge himself against the world's best, and they played in Europe. Two clubs wanted to sign him. PSV Eindhoven in the Netherlands and Borussia Dortmund in Germany competed for his signature.

Christian opted for the stronger competition in Germany's top league, the Bundesliga, and signed with Dortmund. He was only 16. It was tough to leave home for a foreign country. But that's what he decided to do to pursue his dream of becoming one of the greatest soccer players in the world.

Christian took his talents to Germany at a young age.

DORTMUND
DYNAMO

Still a teenager, Christian began his Dortmund career in the club's youth academy. He began playing on Dortmund's U-17 team in 2015 at age 16. It didn't take long for him to fit in.

Christian only played eight matches with the U-17 team. In those eight matches, he racked up six goals and five assists. Then it was on to the U-19 team. Christian netted four goals and added three assists in his first seven games with that squad.

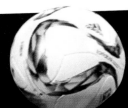

Christian fights off an Ingolstadt defender while making his Bundesliga debut in January 2016.

Pulisic is congratulated by teammate Felix Passlack after scoring his first Bundesliga goal for Dortmund.

There was nothing left to prove at the youth level. The next stop was Dortmund's senior team. Christian had flown through the ranks in less than a year. He made his senior team debut at age 17 on January 30, 2016. He came on as a substitute in the 68th minute against Ingolstadt.

By February, Christian was in the starting lineup. He failed to score, but he had several chances. In a game against Schalke, he created an opportunity out of nothing. He received a pass between two defenders. He bounced the ball off his head twice to get space to run free. Then he fired the ball at the goal, just barely missing the far post.

Christian finally broke through in April. He started Dortmund's match with Hamburg on April 17. In the 38th minute, a teammate flicked the ball to him in the box. Christian took a step inside, then took a shot. With just a few feet of open net, he buried the chance.

He was 17 years, six months, and 30 days old. That made him the youngest foreign player ever to score in the Bundesliga. The goal showed Christian was not just a prospect in Germany. He was on the way to international stardom.

AMERICAN ABROAD

Located in the Ruhr region of western Germany, Borussia Dortmund is one of the country's biggest teams. More than 80,000 fans pack its famous Westfalenstadion for each game. What stood out to Christian, however, was the club's reputation for developing talented young players. Among them were Mario Götze of Germany and Ousmane Dembélé of France. "I kind of knew it was the right place for me," Christian said in 2016, "and it's been the best decision."

STARS AND
STRIPES

Christian has often been one of the youngest players on his teams. It was the case at Dortmund. And it was the case for the US national teams.

Christian began his international career on the US U-15 team in 2012, when he was only 13. On a team of older players, Christian was the standout. He scored 21 goals in 28 games. He spent two seasons with the U-15s before moving up to the U-17 team in 2013. In 2015 Christian was named to the US team for the U-17 World Cup. He scored the opening goal in a 2–2 tie with Croatia.

Christian's experience playing with older teammates and opponents helped when he joined the US U-17 team as a 15-year-old.

NO. 10

Jersey No. 10 has a huge meaning in soccer. It is often worn by a team's top playmaker. It has huge meaning for US soccer fans, too. Landon Donovan wore No. 10 for the United States. He is among the greatest players in American soccer history. Within six months of being called up to the national team, Christian was assigned No. 10. It signified the high hopes coaches had for him.

The spring of 2016 was a remarkable time for Christian. Soon after he joined the Dortmund starting lineup, he got exciting news. US national team manager Jürgen Klinsmann called him up for a pair of World Cup qualifying matches. Christian did not play in the first one due to illness. But he made his national team debut against Guatemala on March 29.

Christian spent most of the match on the bench. His American teammates dominated Guatemala. But in the 81st minute, he got his chance. Christian entered the game to replace Graham Zusi. It was historic. At 17 years old, Pulisic became the youngest US player in World Cup qualifying history.

Christian was ready when he got the call to make his US national team debut against Guatemala in March 2016.

But Christian wanted to do more than come on as a substitute. He wanted to start matches. He wanted to score goals. Fortunately for him—and for US soccer fans— his time was coming.

MOVING UP AND
MOVING ON

After his rapid rise with Dortmund, Christian began his first full season in the Bundesliga in 2016–17. In one week in September, he became Dortmund's youngest player to take part in the Champions League and scored his first Bundesliga goal of the season. A few days after that, he turned 18.

Pulisic's decision to move to Germany was paying off. In January, he signed a contract extension. It was scheduled to keep him with Dortmund until 2020. The German team saw him as a building block for the future.

Christian celebrates his first goal of the season for Dortmund in September 2016.

Pulisic was developing into a dangerous winger for Dortmund. That showed against Europe's best in the Champions League. In March, he scored his first goal in the competition. He was the youngest ever to do so for Dortmund. Pulisic helped Dortmund reach the quarterfinals. And the team finished third in the Bundesliga.

His rise in the sport came at a key time. Back home, Pulisic's national team needed him. The summer of 2017 was a vital stretch for the Americans. Pulisic's two goals against Trinidad and Tobago kept the team's World Cup qualifying hopes alive. But they needed more.

The last two World Cup qualifying matches were against Panama and Trinidad and Tobago. Wins in both would clinch a spot for the United States. Pulisic got them off to a hot start against Panama, scoring in the eighth minute. The Americans won 4–0.

Pulisic was there again in Trinidad. The United States trailed 2–0. Pulisic fired home a perfectly placed ball in

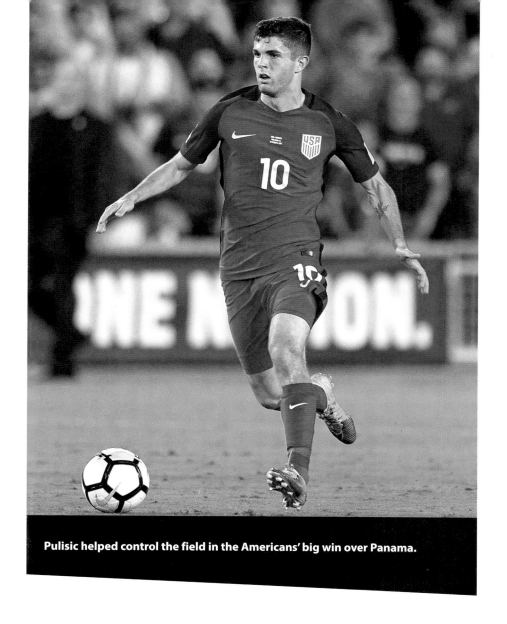

Pulisic helped control the field in the Americans' big win over Panama.

the top corner of the net just after halftime. The Americans were still losing. But based on the results of the other matches, they still were in position to qualify.

Pulisic and his teammates were inconsolable after losing in Trinidad.

But those results changed in an instant. Suddenly the Americans needed at least a draw, or they were out of the World Cup. Pulisic tried to lead the team to get a tying goal. But they could not do it. After the match, Pulisic wiped away tears with his jersey. He was determined not to let the team fail again.

Missing the World Cup was a major blow to the US team. Pulisic's future, however, remained bright. People around Europe saw the success he was having at Dortmund. Some of the biggest clubs in the world wanted to sign him. In 2019, Chelsea did just that. The English power paid Dortmund $73.1 million to sign Pulisic. That was the biggest transfer fee ever for an American player. He agreed to join the London team at the start of the next season.

Pulisic had shown he was no ordinary player. He was a difference maker for both his club and his country. But he still had much more he wanted to accomplish for both.

ONE OF THE BEST

Pulisic and the United States may have failed to qualify for the 2018 World Cup. But Pulisic himself showed he belongs among the world's best. Pulisic was named one of the 11 best players in the region for 2017. He was the top scorer in the fifth round of World Cup qualifying with five goals.

GLOSSARY

assists
Passes that lead directly to goals.

Champions League
An interleague competition for the best club in Europe.

club
The team a player competes with outside of his or her national team.

contract
An agreement to play for a certain team.

debut
First appearance.

dribble
The touches on the ball by a player as it is taken up the field.

midfielder
A player who stays mostly in the middle third of the field and links the defenders with the forwards.

national team
The team that represents a country in international play, such as the World Cup.

qualify
To meet the standard required for entry.

retired
Ended one's career.

substitute
A player who starts the game on the bench but is eligible to enter as a replacement for one of the starters.

transfer fee
The amount of money paid by one club to another for the right to sign one of its players to a contract.

winger
An attacking midfielder who plays wide.

World Cup
The biggest soccer tournament in the world, held once every four years among national teams.

youth academy
A program run by a club to train young players and help them improve their skills.

MORE INFORMATION

BOOKS

Jökulsson, Illugi. *U.S.A. Men's Team: Stars on the Field*. New York: Abbeville Press Publishers, 2014.

Killion, Ann. *Champions of Men's Soccer*. New York: Philomel Books, 2018.

Zweig, Eric. *Absolute Expert: Soccer*. Washington, DC: National Geographic, 2018.

ONLINE RESOURCES

Booklinks
NONFICTION NETWORK
FREE! ONLINE NONFICTION RESOURCES

To learn more about Christian Pulisic, please visit **abdobooklinks.com** or scan this QR code. These links are routinely monitored and updated to provide the most current information available.

INDEX

ABOUT THE AUTHOR

Todd Kortemeier is a sportswriter, editor, children's book author, and soccer fan from Minnesota. A die-hard Tottenham Hotspur supporter, he lives near Minneapolis with his wife and dog.